ABOUT THE AUTHOR

The immense value of the teachings of His Holiness the Dalai Lama have made him, with Mahatma Gandhi, Mother Teresa and Pope John Paul II, one of the genuinely transcendent spiritual figures of our age. Like these three remarkable teachers, the Dalai Lama has been able to reach beyond his Buddhist devotees to find a universal relevance. Those who revere him do not necessarily adopt Buddhist practices but virtually all derive spiritual and mental enrichment from his insights on daily living, inner peace, compassion, peace and justice.

The Little Book of Wisdom is a timeless collection of advice, comment and sayings from one of the world's most widely known and admired spiritual leaders. It is drawn from a longer work called *The Dalai Lama's Book of Wisdom*, which is also available from Rider, as is *The Dalai Lama's Book of Daily Meditations*.

THE LITTLE BOOK OF
WISDOM
Change your outlook
one day at a time

HIS HOLINESS THE
DALAI LAMA

LONDON · SYDNEY · AUCKLAND · JOHANNESBURG

5 7 9 10 8 6 4

Rider, an imprint of Ebury Publishing,
20 Vauxhall Bridge Road,
London SW1V 2SA

Rider is part of the Penguin Random House group of companies whose
addresses can be found at global.penguinrandomhouse.com

Penguin
Random House
UK

Copyright © Matthew E. Bunson 1997

Matthew E. Bunson has asserted his right to be identified
as the author of this Work in accordance with the
Copyright, Designs and Patents Act 1988

First published by Rider in 1997
This edition published in 2018
www.penguin.co.uk

A CIP catalogue record for this book is available from the British Library

ISBN 9781846045622

Printed and bound in Great Britain by Clays Ltd, Elcograf S.p.A.

Penguin Random House is committed to a sustainable future for
our business, our readers and our planet. This book is made
from Forest Stewardship Council® certified paper.

MIX
Paper from
responsible sources
FSC® C018179

SPIRITUAL LIFE

LOVE SPRINGS ETERNAL

The foundation of all spiritual
practice is love.

MEDITATE ON THE TRUTH

If we can realise and meditate on
ultimate truth, it will cleanse our
impurities of mind and thus eradicate
the sense of discrimination.

MEDITATION

Meditation should form
the basis for action.

ULTIMATE TRUTH

In the search for ultimate truth, if it fails
to dawn on us, it is we who have not
found it. Ultimate truth exists. If we think
deeply and reflect carefully, we shall
realise that we ourselves have
our existence in ultimate truth.

RENUNCIATION

It is said that we should renounce this
life. That doesn't mean that we should go
hungry or not take care of this lifetime
at all, but that we should reduce our
attachment to affairs that are
limited to this lifetime.

INNER QUIET

If, inside, you possess good qualities, such
as compassion or spiritual forgiveness ...
then external factors will not affect the
internal peace of the mind.

KINDNESS BRING ABOUT PEACE

With kindness, with love and
compassion, with this feeling that
is the essence of brotherhood,
sisterhood, one will have inner peace.

SPIRITUAL PROGRESS

We must take direct responsibility for our
own spiritual lives and rely upon nobody
and nothing ... If another being were
able to save us, surely he would already
have done so? It is time, therefore,
that we help ourselves.

THE SEEDS OF SPIRITUALITY

The essence of all spiritual life is your emotion, your attitude towards others. Once you have pure and sincere motivation, all the rest follows.

THE SOURCE OF SPIRITUALITY

The dominant force of our mind is
compassion and human affection.
Therefore. I call these human
qualities spirituality.

SPIRITUALITY OUTSIDE OF RELIGION

Without accepting a religion, but simply developing a realisation of the importance of compassion and love, and with more concern and respect for others, a kind of spiritual development is very possible for those persons who are outside of religion.

THE INNER JOURNEY

Purifying the mind is not easy.
It takes a lot of time and hard work ...
You need tremendous willpower and
determination right from the start,
accepting that there will be many
obstacles, and resolving that despite
them all you will continue until you
have attained your goal.

PRACTISE LOVE

To do so in all situations will take time,
but you should not lose courage.
If we wish happiness for mankind,
love is the only way.

HAPPINESS LIES WITHIN

The very purpose of our life is happiness:
in order to achieve happier days, happier
weeks, happier years, happier family,
happier human community ... we should
pay more attention to inner development.

CHARACTERISTICS OF THE EVOLVED INDIVIDUAL

We need human qualities such as moral scruples, compassion and humility ... These qualities are accessible only through forceful individual development.

FOR THE GOOD OF ALL

Even if only a few individuals try to create
mental peace and happiness within
themselves and act responsibly and kind-
heartedly towards others, they will have a
positive influence in their community.

FACING PROBLEMS

If, despite external difficulties or problems,
internally one's attitude is of love, warmth
and kind-heartedness, then problems can
be faced and accepted easily.

HUMILITY

If one assumes a humble attitude, one's
own good qualities will increase.

RESPECT FOR OTHERS

By developing a sense of respect for
others and a concern for their welfare,
we reduce our own selfishness, which is
the source of all problems, and enhance
our sense of kindness, which is a natural
source of goodness.

ACHIEVING A QUIET MIND

Since even wild animals can gradually
be trained with patience, the human
mind also can gradually be
trained, step by step.

LOVE AND PEACE

Inner tranquillity comes from the
development of love and compassion.

SELF-DEVELOPMENT

TAKE CONTROL

To make the mind docile, it is essential for
us to discipline and control it well.

TRAINING THE MIND

Just as a trainer disciplines and calms
a wild and wilful steed by subjecting it
to skilful and prolonged training, so must
the wild, wandering, random activities of
body and speech be tamed to make
them docile, righteous and skilful.

SELF MASTERY

If someone who easily gets angry tries
to control his or her anger, in time it
can be controlled. The same is true
for a very selfish person.

THOUGHTS SHAPE EVENTS

All things first originate in the mind. Things
and events depend heavily on motivation.

THE IMPORTANCE
OF MOTIVATION

The prime mover of every human action
is motivation ... Our motivation should be
simple and sincere. Whether we achieve
the goal or not does not matter so long
as our motivation is very sincere
and we make the attempt.

LEARN FROM YOUR ENEMY

It is the enemy who can try and teach
us to practise the virtues of compassion
and tolerance. You can learn about the
importance of being patient. However, the
actual practice of implementing patience
comes when meeting with an enemy.

OVERCOMING
DIFFICULTIES

Tolerance is very important. If you have
tolerance, you can easily overcome
difficulties. If you have little tolerance
or are without it, then the smallest
thing immediately irritates you.

THE HUMAN COST OF
CONSUMER CULTURE

One of the principal factors that
hinder us from fully appreciating our
interdependence is our undue emphasis
on material development. We have
become so engrossed in its pursuit that,
unknowingly, we have neglected the
most basic qualities of compassion,
caring and cooperation.

STRIKE A BALANCE

There should be a balance between
material and spiritual progress, a balance
achieved through the principles based
on love and compassion.

THE KEY TO SUCCESS

Determination, with an optimistic attitude,
is the key factor for success.

INNER VISIONS
CREATE OUTER REALITY

If we want a beautiful garden, we
must first have a blueprint in the
imagination, a vision. Then that idea
can be implemented and the external
garden can be materialised.

ANALYSE YOUR
THOUGHTS ...

When we talk about the inner world,
there are a lot of different thoughts, or
different minds ... Those thoughts and
actions which ultimately bring happiness,
they are positive. Those thoughts and
actions which ultimately bring
suffering, they are negative.

... THEN FOCUS
ON THE POSITIVE

Through mental training you can increase
these positive thoughts and can reduce
negative thoughts. I can tell you with
conviction, through effort we can
change our mental attitude.

HAPPINESS

THE PURPOSE OF LIFE

Whether we are rich or poor, educated
or uneducated, whatever our nationality,
colour, social status or ideology may be,
the purpose of our lives is to be happy.

STRIVING AFTER
WORLDLY SUCCESS

If striving thus were really productive
of permanent happiness, then among
the many people in this world endowed
with power, wealth and friendship, there
would surely be some blessed with a large
measure of real and lasting happiness.

HAPPINESS CAN'T
BE BOUGHT

Mental peace cannot be injected
by any doctor; no market can sell
mental peace or happiness.

PEACE LIES WITHIN

We are trying to get peace or
happiness from outside, from money
or power. But real peace, tranquillity,
should come from within.

THE KEY TO FULFILMENT

Unless our minds are stable and calm,
no matter how comfortable our physical
condition may be, they will give us no
pleasure. Therefore, the key to a happy
life, now and in the future, is to
develop a happy mind.

AS YOU SOW, SO YOU REAP

Happiness comes from kindness.
Happiness cannot come from
hatred or anger.

THE RIPPLE EFFECT

If an individual human being eventually
becomes a nice, calm, peaceful person,
then it automatically brings some kind
of positive atmosphere, and you
have a happy family.

LOVE AND COMPASSION

LOVE IS THE CENTRE
OF HUMAN LIFE

Love and compassion ... are the ultimate
source of human happiness, and our need
for them lies at the very core of our being.

A GOOD HEART

A good mind, a good heart, warm feelings
– these are the most important things.

REAL LOVE

Real love is not based on attachment.

LOVE DOES NOT DISCRIMINATE

The kind of love we advocate is the love you can have even for someone who has done harm to you. This kind of love is to be extended to all living beings, and it can be extended to all living beings.

LOVE IS HARD

Compassion and love are precious things
in life. They are not complicated. They are
simple, but difficult to practise.

LOVE YOUR ENEMY

If you have love and compassion toward
all sentient beings, particularly toward
your enemy, that is true love
and compassion.

THE GREATNESS
OF MATERNAL LOVE

The feeling of a mother for her child is a classic example of love. For the safety, protection and welfare of her children, a mother is ready to sacrifice her very life.

LOVE ONE ANOTHER

Human beings are social creatures,
and a concern for each other is the
very basis of our life together.

LOVE'S CONSOLATION

Love ... consoles when one is helpless
and distressed, and it consoles when one
is old and lonely. It is a dynamic force
that we should develop and use, but
often tend to neglect, particularly in our
prime years, when we experience a
false sense of security.

DO AS YOU WOULD
BE DONE BY

Since at the beginning and end of our
lives we are so dependent on others'
kindness, how can it be that in the middle
we neglect kindness towards others.

THE MORE YOU GIVE,
THE MORE YOU RECEIVE

The more we care for the happiness
of others, the greater is our own
sense of well-being.

LOVE CONQUERS ALL

Cultivating a close, warm-hearted feeling
for others automatically puts the mind at
ease and opens our inner door. It helps
remove whatever fears or insecurities we
may have and gives us the strength to
cope with any obstacles we encounter.
It is the principal source of success in life.

LOVE IS ALWAYS
APPROPRIATE

Love and kindness are always appropriate.
Whether or not you believe in rebirth, you
will need love in this life. If we have love,
there is hope to have real families, real
brotherhood, real equanimity, real peace.

EVERY ONE OF US
HAS THE CAPACITY
FOR KINDNESS

The development of a kind heart, or
feeling of closeness for all human beings,
does not involve any of the kind of
religiosity we normally associate with it ...
It is for everyone, irrespective of race,
religion or any political affiliation.

THE WAY FORWARD

As a human being, kindness, a warm
heart, is very important ... If you have this
basic quality of kindness or good heart,
then all other things, education, ability,
will go in the right direction.

PUT OTHERS FIRST

Our doings and thinkings must be
motivated by compassion for others.
The way to acquire that kind of outlook
is to accept the simple fact that whatever
we desire is also desired by others.

GENUINE COMPASSION

Genuine compassion is unbiased,
should be unbiased.

COMPASSION IS
BORN OF RESPECT

Genuine compassion must be acting on
the basis of respect, and the realisation
or recognition that others also, just like
myself, have the right to be happy.

COMPASSION
REACHES OUT TO ALL

Compassion compels us to reach out to all living beings, including our so-called enemies, those people who upset or hurt us. Irrespective of what they do to you, if you remember that all beings like you are only trying to be happy, you will find it much easier to develop compassion towards them.

COMPASSION IS A SIGN
OF INNER STRENGTH

Compassion is, by nature, peaceful and
gentle, but it is also very powerful.

FINDING YOUR WAY

Each of us in our own way can try to
spread compassion into people's hearts.

COMPASSION
IS RESPONSIBLE

To experience genuine compassion
is to develop a feeling of closeness
to others combined with a sense of
responsibility for their welfare.

COMPASSION
IS COMMITTED

True compassion is not just an
emotional response but a firm
commitment founded on reason.

COMPASSION
IS CONSTANT

A truly compassionate attitude
towards others does not change,
even if they behave negatively.

THE INNER ENEMIES

THE ENEMY
IN YOUR HEART

There is one enemy who is always an enemy, with whom you should never compromise; that is the enemy inside your heart. You cannot change all these bad thoughts into your friend, but you have to confront and control them.

THE ROOT OF
ALL PROBLEMS

Anger, attachment, jealousy, hatred ...
these are the real enemy.

NEGATIVITY IS
NEVER THE SOLUTION

Anger, jealousy, impatience and hatred
are the real troublemakers; with them
problems cannot be solved. Though one
may have temporary success, ultimately
one's hatred or anger will create
further difficulties.

NO GOOD EVER
CAME OF ANGER

Anger may seem to offer an energetic
way of getting things done, but such a
perception of the world is misguided.
The only certainty about anger and
hatred is that they are destructive.

TWO KINDS OF ANGER

Anger I think can be of two types: hatred
with ill-feeling is one while another anger
— with compassion as the basis of
concern — may be positive.

KEEP ANGER IN CHECK

Usually people consider that anger is part
of the mind, and that it is better to show
it, to let it come. I think that's the wrong
conception ... Resentment because of
grievances may be let out, because
then it is finished ... Constant anger
– that, I think, it is better to check.

TWO WRONGS
DON'T MAKE A RIGHT

Hatred cannot be overcome by hatred ...
Hatred will only generate more problems.

FEAR

Fear arises when we view
everyone else with suspicion.

THE PATH TO
SELF-DESTRUCTION

If we live our lives continually
motivated by anger and hatred, even
our physical health deteriorates.

VIOLENCE IS
SELF-PERPETUATING

If you succeed through violence at the
expense of others' rights and welfare, you
have not solved the problem, but only
created the seeds for another.

SELF-IMPORTANCE

Tolerance and patience with courage
are not signs of failure but signs of victory
... Actually, if you are too important,
that's a real failure.

MORAL VALUES

CAUSE AND EFFECT

One's own actions create
one's life situation.

THE POWER OF LOVE

A good heart is both important
and effective in daily life.

REAPING THE BENEFITS

The reason why we seek to behave in
a good manner is that it's from good
behaviour that good fruits are derived.

BUILDING A BETTER LIFE

One wants happiness and doesn't
want suffering, and on the basis of that,
one enters into good actions and
avoids bad actions.

GUIDING PRINCIPLES

Be guided by realism,
moderation, and patience.

WORK FOR THE
WELFARE OF ALL

With a pure heart, you can carry
on any work ... and your profession
becomes a real instrument to help
the human community.

PURITY OF INTENTION

Once you have pure and sincere
motivation, all the rest follows. You can
develop this right attitude towards others
on the basis of kindness, love and respect,
and on the clear realisation of the
oneness of all human beings.

CARING FOR OTHERS

Most of the good or beneficial effects
that come about in the world are based
on an attitude of cherishing others.
The opposite is also true.

GIVE AND TAKE

By showing concern for other people's
welfare, sharing other people's suffering,
and helping other people, ultimately
one will benefit. If one thinks only of
oneself and forgets about others,
ultimately one will lose.

LOOK AHEAD

It is more important to look forward to
the future than dwell in the past.

THE PARADOX
OF SELF-INTEREST

If we adopt a self-centred approach to
life by which we attempt to use others for
our own self-interest, we might be able to
gain temporary benefit, but in the long
run we will not succeed in achieving
even our personal happiness.

OPTIMISM ACHIEVES GREATNESS

An optimistic attitude is the key factor
for success. Right from the beginning,
if you hold a pessimistic attitude even
small things may not be achieved.

SIGNS OF SUCCESS

In your daily life, as you learn more
patience, more tolerance with wisdom
and courage, you will see it is the
true source of success.

GOOD COMMUNICATIONS

Compassion ... opens an inner door,
and once through the door we can
communicate with other fellow human
beings and other sentient beings.

TEACH BY EXAMPLE

Before teaching others, before changing others, we ourselves must change. We must be honest, sincere, kind-hearted.

DO AS YOU WOULD
BE DONE BY

We should share the sufferings of our
fellow human beings and practise
compassion and tolerance, not only
towards our loved ones but
towards our enemies.

WORK FOR THE
WELFARE OF OTHERS

Our daily thoughts and actions should be
directed towards the benefit of others.

PRACTISE WHAT
YOU PREACH

We should engage in the same
high standards of integrity and
sacrifice that we ask of others.

DON'T BE SEDUCED
BY WORLDLY VALUES

Materialism does not foster the growth
of morals, compassion and humility.

TAKE RESPONSIBILITY
FOR THOSE IN NEED

It is the nature of human beings to
yearn for freedom, equality and dignity.
If we accept that others have a right to
peace and happiness equal to our own,
do we not have a responsibility
to help those in need?

TAKE ACTION

No one can afford to assume that someone else will solve our problems. Every individual has a responsibility to help guide our human family in the right direction. Good wishes are not sufficient.

THE MORAL CODE

Irrespective of whether we are a believer
or an agnostic, whether we believe in God
or karma, moral ethics is a code which
everyone is able to pursue.

THE MORAL PERSPECTIVE

To pursue growth properly, we need to
renew our commitment to human values
in many fields. Political life, of course,
requires an ethical foundation, but science
and religion as well should be pursued
from a moral basis.

FAMILY
& FRIENDS

TRUE FRIENDSHIP

The proper way to create friends is
through a warm heart and not simple
money or power. Friends of power
and friends of money are something
different. These are not friends.

MAKING FRIENDS

If we have a kind and loving heart
we will win more friends.

BE FRIENDLY

Friends are very important, as are a
friendly manner and a genuine smile.

SMILE FROM THE HEART

A genuine smile must come from
the face of compassion.

MUTUAL INTEREST

If you want friends and a friendly
atmosphere, you must create the basis
for them. Whether the other's response will
be positive or not, first you must create
some kind of common ground.

CREATE A PEACEFUL ENVIRONMENT

If in a small family, even without children, the members have a warm heart to each other, a peaceful atmosphere will be created. However, if one of the persons feels angry, immediately the atmosphere in the house becomes tense.

CHERISH ONE ANOTHER

If we cherish others, then both others and
ourselves, both deeply and superficially,
will be happy ... When we cherish
ourselves more than others ... we
produce various types of suffering,
both for ourselves and for
those around us.

LIVING IN HARMONY

Peaceful living is about trusting those
on whom we depend and caring for
those who depend on us.

BE FORGIVING

When we are able to recognise and
forgive ignorant actions of the past, we
gain the strength to solve the problems
of the past constructively.

COMPASSION
BUILDS TRUST

It is compassion that creates the sense
of trust that allows us to open up to
others and reveal our problems,
doubts and uncertainties.

HOW CHILDREN THRIVE

Children whose homes have love and
affection are better, healthier, normal
and sturdy. Where children lack human
affection and love, physical development
is sometimes difficult, as is study.

CHILDHOOD DEPRIVATION

Children who had difficulties at an early age, growing under a lack of human love and affection, will find it difficult to show other humans love and compassion. And that's a great tragedy, a great tragedy.

BUDDHISM

LOVE AND COMPASSION

The essence of Buddhism is kindness,
compassion. This is the essence
of every religion.

ALL ARE EQUAL

Central to the Buddha's teaching is
seeing the equality among humanity and
the importance of equality of all sentient
beings. Whether you are a Buddhist or
not, this is something important to
know and understand.

AVOID INJURY TO OTHERS

Destruction or injury to life is strictly
forbidden. Harming or destroying any
being from the highest to the lowest,
from a human to the tiniest insect,
must at all costs be avoided.

ACTIONS SPEAK
LOUDER THAN WORDS

Merely to call oneself a
Buddhist is of little value.

THE BUDDHA'S TEACHINGS

The Buddha himself taught different
things according to the place, the
occasion and the situation of those
who were listening to him.

REAL CHANGE TAKES
PLACE ON THE INSIDE

If you have adopted Buddhism you
should not consider yourself a 'great
Buddhist' and immediately start to do
everything differently. A Tibetan proverb
states, 'Change your mind but leave
your appearance as usual.'

ABSOLUTE TRUTH

From the viewpoint of absolute truth,
what we feel and experience in our
ordinary daily life is all delusion.

THE HUMAN CONDITION

All other beings are just like us in that they want happiness and dislike suffering.

THE UNIVERSALITY
OF SUFFERING

Every single one of us – be he a ruler
or warrior, be he rich, middle-class, or
poor – is subject to all sorts of physical
and mental suffering, especially
torments of the mind.

THE ULTIMATE DELUSION

Of all the various delusions, the sense of
discrimination between oneself and others
is the worst form, as it creates nothing but
unpleasantness for both sides.

RELIGION

MANY WAYS, ONE TRUTH

Despite the differences in the names
and forms used by the various religions,
the ultimate truth to which they
point is the same.

TOLERANCE

Practitioners of different faiths should realise that each religious tradition has immense intrinsic value as a means for providing mental and spiritual health.

A GOOD HEART

Religion is not something outside,
but in our hearts. The essence of
any religion is a good heart.

THE VEHICLES OF TRUTH

No one religion is appropriate for all types of people. Just as Buddhism is not best for everyone, Christianity is not appropriate for all types of disposition.

FOOD FOR THOUGHT

Religion is a food for the mind, and as
we all have different tastes, we must take
that which is most suitable for us.

THE ROLE OF RELIGION

Western civilisations these days place
great importance on filling the human
brain with knowledge, but no one seems
to care about filling the human heart
with compassion. This is what the
real role of religion is.

PRACTICE IS MORE IMPORTANT THAN THEORY

It is much more beneficial to try to implement daily the shared precepts for goodness taught by all religions rather than to argue about minor differences in approach.

LIVE BY YOUR BELIEFS

All major religions are basically the same
in that they emphasise peace of mind
and kindness, but it is very important to
practise this in our daily lives, not
just in a church or temple.

THE GOAL OF RELIGION

The purpose of religion is not to build
beautiful churches or temples, but to
cultivate positive human qualities, such
as tolerance, generosity and love.

THE COMMONALITY
OF ALL RELIGIONS

Every religion of the world has similar
ideals of love, the same goal of benefiting
humanity through spiritual practice, and
the same effect of making its followers
into better human beings ... Each, in its
own way, teaches a path leading to
a spiritual state that is peaceful,
disciplined, ethical and wise.

PURITY OF HEART

If the motivation is sincere, then every
human action can be positive – including
political initiatives. If our motivation is not
adequate, not pure, even religion
becomes smeared.

TAKING THE NAME OF
RELIGION IN VAIN

Sometimes in the name of religion people
cause more quarrels than they solve.

WORLD PEACE

THE BASIS
FOR WORLD PEACE

Genuine peace, genuine lasting
world peace, can be achieved
only through inner peace.

UNIVERSAL
RESPONSIBILITY

Universal responsibility is the key
to human survival. It is the best
foundation for world peace.

THE EXTERNAL
WORLD REFLECTS
OUR INNER REALITIES

The well-being of society ... depends
upon the internal attitude of the
people who compose it.

INGREDIENTS FOR PEACE

Through kindness ... through mutual
understanding and through mutual respect
we will get peace, we will get happiness,
and we will get genuine satisfaction.

PRACTISE KINDNESS

It is very difficult to achieve peace
and harmony through competition and
hatred, so the practice of kindness is
very, very important and very, very
valuable in human society.

LOVE AND COMPASSION

Love and compassion are the
moral fabric of world peace.

GLOBAL ISSUES

UNNECESSARY SUFFERING

Humans must face death, old age
and disease as well as natural disasters,
such as hurricanes, that are beyond our
control ... But these sufferings are quite
sufficient for us. Why should we create
other problems due to our own ideology,
just different ways of thinking?

GLOBAL CHANGE BEGINS
WITH INDIVIDUAL ACTION

For any change, and movement in the
human community, the initiative
must come from individuals.

UNIVERSAL BENEFITS

When we are motivated by wisdom and compassion, the results of our actions benefit everyone, not just our individual selves or some immediate convenience.

MUTUAL INTERESTS

The more we become interdependent,
the more it is in our interest to ensure
the well-being of others.

CONCERN FOR OTHERS

When we do not know someone or do not
feel connected to an individual or group,
we tend to overlook their needs. Yet the
development of human society requires
that people help each other.

ETHICS IN PUBLIC LIFE

It is an absurd assumption that religion
and morality have no place in politics.

'WE' AND 'THEY'

The whole world is becoming smaller
and smaller. The concept of 'we'
and 'they' is gone, out of date.

DEATH AND LIBERATION

ETERNAL LIFE

At the moment we are blessed with human
life and with all the possibilities that this
implies ... When we die nothing can be
taken with us but the seeds of our life's
work and our spiritual knowledge.

THE IMPERMANENCE
OF MIND

Since experience and knowledge are
impermanent and subject to disintegration,
the mind of which they are functions
is not something that remains
constant and eternal.

TIME IS PRECIOUS:
USE IT WELL

If we use this human brain for something of little import, that is very sad. If we spend our time just concerned with the affairs of this lifetime up to the point of death, that is very sad and weak.

ULTIMATE DEATH

In ultimate death, if I search for myself
I will not find it, and if you search for
yourselves you will not find them.